McLean County Memories II

The 1940s, 1950s and 1960s • A Pictorial History

presented by

THE PANTAGRAPH

ACKNOWLEDGMENTS

The Pantagraph is pleased to present McLean County Memories II: The 1940s, 1950s and 1960s. It must be noted, however, that this unique pictorial history book would not have been possible without the generous contributions made by many people from virtually every corner of our community.

We are indebted, first of all, to those early area residents who captured their time — our history — in photographs, and provided a glimpse into their lives.

Secondly, all area residents are indebted to the many individuals who are committed to preserving our history in various libraries, historical societies, archives and personal collections throughout our community.

The following organizations have contributed greatly to this project:

Bloomington Public Library
Funk Prairie Home Museum
Illinois State University
McLean County Museum of History
Normal Public Library
Tate Archives & Special Collections, The Ames Library,
Illinois Wesleyan University, Bloomington, Illinois

 ISBN: 978-1-59725-648-3

Published by Pediment Publishing, a division of The Pediment Group, Inc. www.pediment.com. Printed in Canada.

FOREWORD

If a picture is worth a thousand words, "McLean County Memories II" has more to say than a set of door-to-door encyclopedias.

The second volume of The Pantagraph's popular history book series focuses on the 1940s, 1950s and 1960s, offering up-close and personal looks at McLean County views and street scenes, transportation, public service, commerce, industry and agriculture, community, education and recreation and celebrations. These snapshots of history represent individuals, families, churches, schools, businesses and more, and were culled from your private family and business collections, as well as the McLean County Museum of History, the museum's Pantagraph Collection, Pantagraph archives, Illinois State University, Illinois Wesleyan University, Bloomington Public Library and Normal Public Library.

"McLean County Memories II" starts with a chapter of new photographs from our last collection, which focused on the late 1800s through the 1930s. Those images set the stage for the newest offering, where you may find long-ago classmates, grandparents in their heyday, and the people for whom our streets, businesses and schools were named.

The two books cover a wide span of years but a common thread connects them: McLean County and its people are strong and decisive, smart and funny, loving, warm and caring. Above all else, those qualities shine through regardless if the picture was a vacation snapshot captured with a Brownie or a formal portrait taken with an Agfa on a tripod.

It makes sense that a community newspaper would produce a history book. After all, a newspaper produces stories and photographs every day that eventually become our shared history. The Pantagraph and its staff are proud to partner with community groups and Pediment Publishing to present "McLean County Memories II: The 1940s, 1950s and 1960s, a Pictorial History."

Enjoy.

N17340
OZARK

TABLE OF CONTENTS

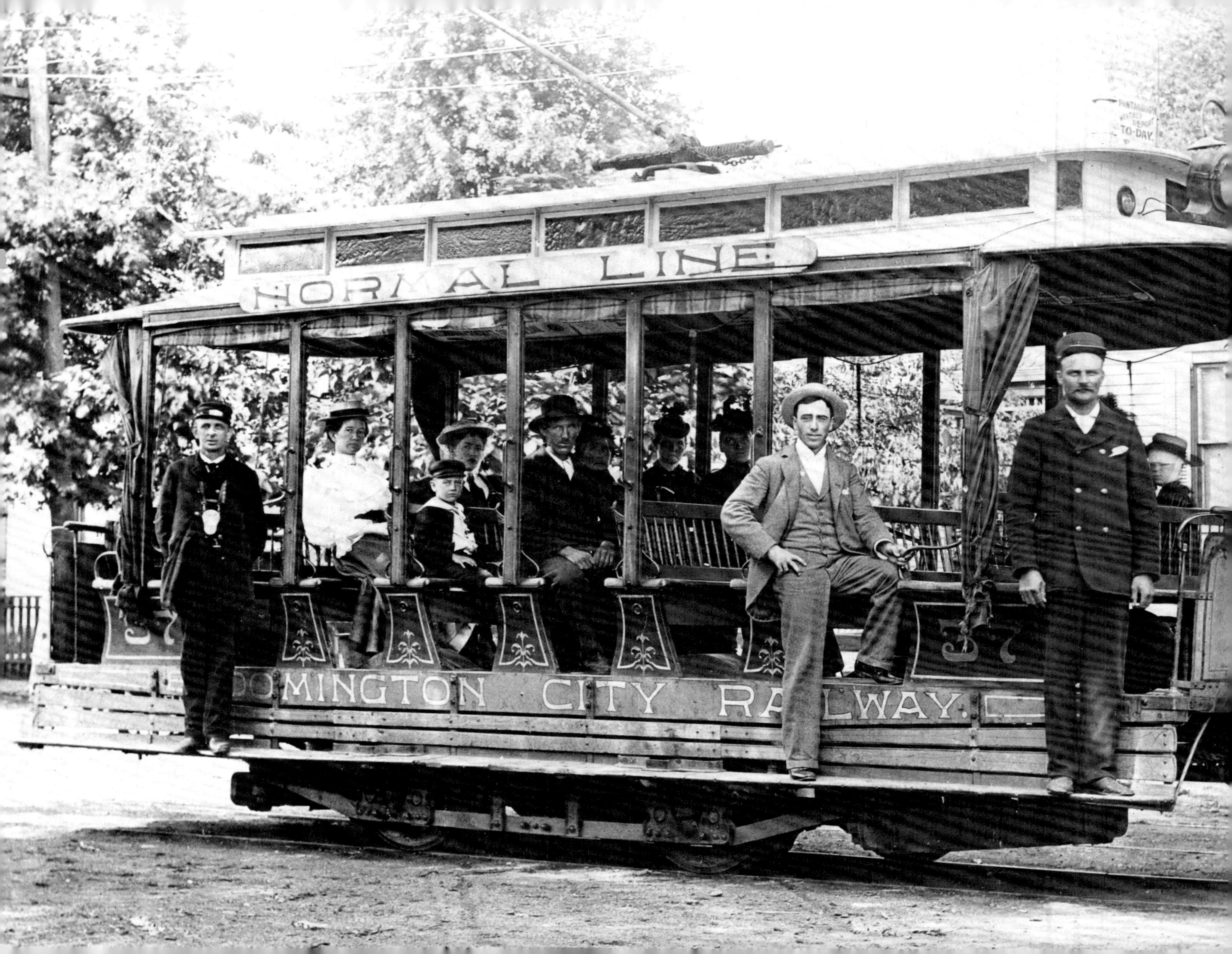

NORMAL LINE
MINGTON CITY RAILWAY.
37
TO-DAY.

CHAPTER ONE

THE EARLY YEARS

The technological and social revolutions that marked the late 1800s and first few decades of the 20th century were in full evidence in McLean County, with advances in transportation, education, construction and more.

The changes were especially noticeable in Bloomington after the Great Fire of 1900 which, in a way, provided a clean slate for the boom chronicled in "McLean County Memories: The Early Years," published by The Pantagraph in December 2015.

The growth (and some contraction) during those early years was felt in all quarters, for although Bloomington and Normal led the way, the smaller communities of McLean County were no strangers to the boom-and-bust period that book-ended the years of the Great Depression.

Those adjustments, and the advent of World War II, paved the way for McLean County's mid-century modernists.

OPPOSITE: The Bloomington-Normal street car, 1905. COURTESY OF THE MCLEAN COUNTY MUSEUM OF HISTORY, PANTAGRAPH COLLECTION

ABOVE: Kadgihn News and Cigars on North Main Street, Bloomington, 1914.
COURTESY OF THE MCLEAN COUNTY MUSEUM OF HISTORY, PANTAGRAPH COLLECTION

ABOVE RIGHT: Looking east on Washington Street, Bloomington, circa 1900.
COURTESY OF THE MCLEAN COUNTY MUSEUM OF HISTORY, PANTAGRAPH COLLECTION

RIGHT: Illinois Wesleyan University's 1914 men's basketball team.
COURTESY TATE ARCHIVES & SPECIAL COLLECTIONS, THE AMES LIBRARY, ILLINOIS WESLEYAN UNIVERSITY, BLOOMINGTON, ILLINOIS

OPPOSITE: Chenoa High School girl's basketball team, 1904.
COURTESY CAROLYN PARRY

C. H. S
1904

ABOVE: Home Sweet Home City Mission providing food at 212 South Main Street, Bloomington, 1925. COURTESY HOME SWEET HOME MINISTRIES

ABOVE LEFT: Students at Illinois State Normal University, circa 1927. COURTESY OF THE MCLEAN COUNTY MUSEUM OF HISTORY, PANTAGRAPH COLLECTION

LEFT: Home Sweet Home City Mission picnic at Miller Park, Bloomington, 1921. COURTESY HOME SWEET HOME MINISTRIES

OPPOSITE: Emerson School eighth-grade graduating class, Clayton Street, Bloomington, 1925. Back row, third from right is Robert Elkenberry. COURTESY JIM & CONNIE TAYLOR

MOTHER
CLEANSING SODA

LEFT: Unitarian church on East Street, Bloomington, circa 1928.
COURTESY OF THE MCLEAN COUNTY MUSEUM OF HISTORY, PANTAGRAPH COLLECTION

OPPOSITE TOP: Mayor Ben Rhodes with his advisors in Bloomington, 1929.
COURTESY OF THE MCLEAN COUNTY MUSEUM OF HISTORY, PANTAGRAPH COLLECTION

OPPOSITE BOTTOM: Donation of food from employees of Williams Oil-O-Matic at Home Sweet Home City Mission, 212 South Main Street, Bloomington, 1930.
COURTESY HOME SWEET HOME MINISTRIES

RIGHT: Glenn C. Miller, R. Dale Miller, and Ray L. Miller of Dale Miller's Orchestra, Bloomington, 1932. They performed throughout Illinois, St. Louis, Michigan, Indiana, and Iowa.
COURTESY NANCY J. MILLER

OPPOSITE: The McLean County Centennial Celebration, 1930.
COURTESY OF THE MCLEAN COUNTY MUSEUM OF HISTORY, PANTAGRAPH COLLECTION

DRUGS
Gainsborough
HAIR NET
S. S. KRESGE CO. 5-10-25¢
PERFUMES
TOILET ARTICLES

ABOVE: The Bloomington Band in 1932.
COURTESY OF THE MCLEAN COUNTY MUSEUM OF HISTORY, PANTAGRAPH COLLECTION

RIGHT: Jack Valentine, Julia Valentine and David Valentine sitting in a goat carriage, 506 East Cherry Street, 1932. COURTESY JULIA CLEINMARK

LEFT: Marjorie Stubblefield and George R. Morrison testing the vault door at People's Bank, 1932. The door could be opened from the inside in case somebody got trapped.
COURTESY OF THE MCLEAN COUNTY MUSEUM OF HISTORY, PANTAGRAPH COLLECTION

BELOW: Bloomington High School's graduating class of 1933.
COURTESY OF THE MCLEAN COUNTY MUSEUM OF HISTORY, PANTAGRAPH COLLECTION

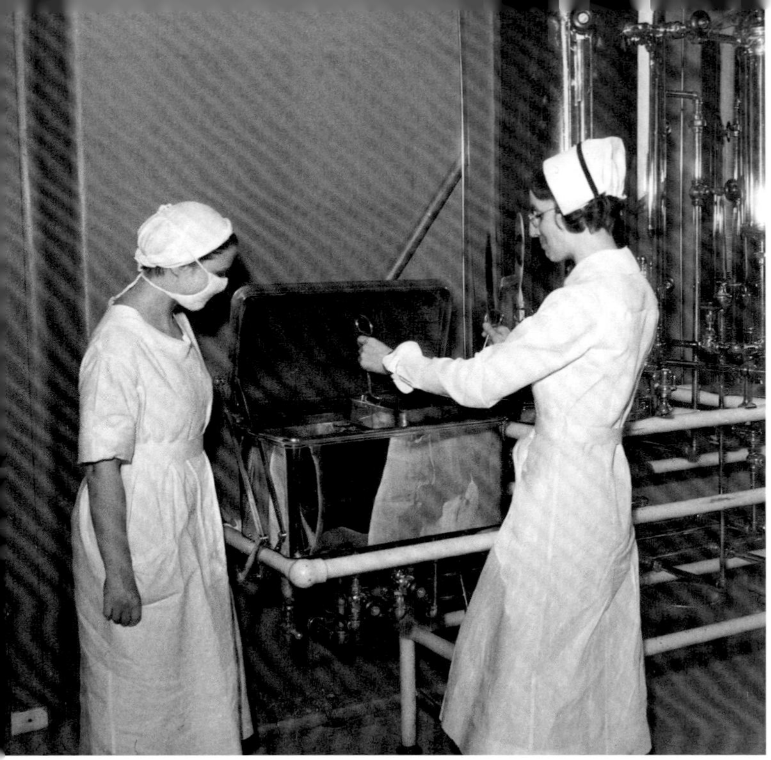

ABOVE: Nurses sterilizing instruments at Brokaw Hospital, Bloomington, 1934.
COURTESY OF THE MCLEAN COUNTY MUSEUM OF HISTORY, PANTAGRAPH COLLECTION

ABOVE RIGHT: Brokaw Hospital's graduating class of 1933.
COURTESY OF THE MCLEAN COUNTY MUSEUM OF HISTORY, PANTAGRAPH COLLECTION

BELOW RIGHT: Candy makers at Paul F. Beich Company in Bloomington, 1934.
COURTESY OF THE MCLEAN COUNTY MUSEUM OF HISTORY, PANTAGRAPH COLLECTION

OPPOSITE LEFT: The Pumpernickel Band, also known as The Spinach Blowers, Bloomington, circa 1933.
COURTESY OF THE MCLEAN COUNTY MUSEUM OF HISTORY, PANTAGRAPH COLLECTION

OPPOSITE TOP RIGHT: A crowd gathering for the Turkey Day celebrations, circa 1939.
COURTESY OF THE MCLEAN COUNTY MUSEUM OF HISTORY, PANTAGRAPH COLLECTION

OPPOSITE BOTTOM RIGHT: Bloomington Airport dedication, 1934.
COURTESY OF THE MCLEAN COUNTY MUSEUM OF HISTORY, PANTAGRAPH COLLECTION

PHOTOS
LUNCH
Coca-Cola

LINCOLN CHAMPIONS
EUREKA CHAMPIONS
SAYBROOK
CHATSWORTH CHAMPIONS
GOODRICH Silvertown Cord
SUPER SERVICE

NEW IDEA

DARLING & CO.
FISH·OYSTERS·POULTRY
DRIVE IN
218

ABOVE: The Soap Box Derby, 1937.
COURTESY OF THE MCLEAN COUNTY MUSEUM OF HISTORY, PANTAGRAPH COLLECTION

LEFT: Bloomington High School pep meet, 1937.
COURTESY OF THE MCLEAN COUNTY MUSEUM OF HISTORY, PANTAGRAPH COLLECTION

OPPOSITE BOTTOM LEFT: New Idea Inc. traveled all the way from Ohio to Bloomington's Alfalfa Day celebration, 1936.
COURTESY OF THE MCLEAN COUNTY MUSEUM OF HISTORY, PANTAGRAPH COLLECTION

OPPOSITE BOTTOM RIGHT: Darling and Company Fish Market, owned by Hugh Darling and located at the corner of Olive and Center streets, circa 1937. COURTESY JIM RETTICK

ABOVE: Mr. and Mrs. Hyer, horse trainers for the circus in Bloomington, 1939.
COURTESY BLOOMINGTON PUBLIC LIBRARY

ABOVE RIGHT: Railroad Week celebrations on Main Street, Bloomington, 1936.
COURTESY OF THE MCLEAN COUNTY MUSEUM OF HISTORY, PANTAGRAPH COLLECTION

RIGHT: The Flying Fishers, Bloomington aerialists in 1937. From left: Charles Fisher, Connie Fisher, Glenn Higginbothen, Edith Fisher, Forest Higginbothen.
COURTESY OF THE MCLEAN COUNTY MUSEUM OF HISTORY, PANTAGRAPH COLLECTION

OPPOSITE: Boy Scouts learning archery in 1938.
COURTESY OF THE MCLEAN COUNTY MUSEUM OF HISTORY, PANTAGRAPH COLLECTION

INGTON BRANCH
ICAGO
OR CLUB

ABOVE: The Bloomington Fire Department's brand new vehicle, 1939.
COURTESY OF THE MCLEAN COUNTY MUSEUM OF HISTORY, PANTAGRAPH COLLECTION

LEFT: The Bloomington Fire Department at the Durley Building fire, 1939.
COURTESY OF THE MCLEAN COUNTY MUSEUM OF HISTORY, PANTAGRAPH COLLECTION

OPPOSITE: Firemen putting out a blaze that caused $125,000 in damage, 1939.
COURTESY OF THE MCLEAN COUNTY MUSEUM OF HISTORY, PANTAGRAPH COLLECTION

ONE OF
ILLINOIS
GREAT STORES
Livingston's
Walgreen
Livingston's
Nunn Bush
SHOES
Bootery

CHAPTER TWO

VIEWS AND STREET SCENES

Cities, schools, churches, businesses and farms grew like gangbusters during the middle of the 20th century, with industry driving tremendous change across the board. Those changes affected types of products and led the way for greater efficiency and increased safety. Factories opened and then expanded. Grain and livestock sales grew as farmers used bigger equipment to work larger parcels and bigger herds with an eye toward commerce, not just sustenance. Jobs and buildings were added, and names changed, at State Farm, Country Companies, General Electric, Eureka-Williams, Kathryn Beich, Beer Nuts and the local hospitals. Higher education opportunities grew and brought with them additional students, teachers, classrooms and dormitory buildings.

Brick streets were covered with asphalt and widened to accommodate more cars, city buses and the Interurban rail system. Smaller, older buildings were expanded or demolished and replaced with taller, broader, bigger structures with flashy peaks, shiny display windows and plenty of storage.

OPPOSITE: Looking east at the 100 block of West Washington Street, Bloomington, 1948. Dewenters, which closed in 1988, can be seen in the lower right.

COURTESY OF THE MCLEAN COUNTY MUSEUM OF HISTORY PANTAGRAPH COLLECTION

ABOVE: An aerial view of Frank Bill's farm outside of Towanda, 1947. COURTESY ROBERT CARMODY

RIGHT: An aerial view of Evergreen Stock Farm located four miles north of Hudson, circa 1940. It was built in the mid-1920s and was used to store thoroughbred racing horses. COURTESY SUE KEERAN

OPPOSITE: A view of LeRoy in February of 1941. COURTESY OF THE MCLEAN COUNTY MUSEUM OF HISTORY, PANTAGRAPH COLLECTION

LAND'S CAFE
Coca-Cola
Budweiser
DRUGS

ABOVE: A view of downtown Normal in May of 1955.
COURTESY ILLINOIS STATE UNIVERSITY

ABOVE RIGHT: A busy Bloomington street in 1955.
COURTESY OF THE MCLEAN COUNTY MUSEUM OF HISTORY, PANTAGRAPH COLLECTION

RIGHT: People in a canoe outside of Briarwood Grocery, 802 East Emerson Street, Normal, 1943. The shop was operated by Chuck Arnold.
COURTESY OF THE MCLEAN COUNTY MUSEUM OF HISTORY, PANTAGRAPH COLLECTION

ABOVE: Two people crossing North Street in downtown Normal, 1955. COURTESY ILLINOIS STATE UNIVERSITY

LEFT: The busy 200 block of East Washington Street in Bloomington prior to the street widening done in 1956. COURTESY OF THE MCLEAN COUNTY MUSEUM OF HISTORY, PANTAGRAPH COLLECTION

ABOVE: Demolition of the old National Bank Building on Washington Street in Bloomington, circa 1959. COURTESY BECKY LEACH O'DONNELL

ABOVE RIGHT: The busy 200 block of East Washington Street after the street widening in 1956. COURTESY OF THE MCLEAN COUNTY MUSEUM OF HISTORY, PANTAGRAPH COLLECTION

RIGHT: A view of the corner of Center and West Washington streets, 1961. COURTESY OF THE MCLEAN COUNTY MUSEUM OF HISTORY, PANTAGRAPH COLLECTION

OPPOSITE: Looking west from the Lafayette Apartments on the 400 block of East Washington Street, circa 1955. COURTESY OF THE MCLEAN COUNTY MUSEUM OF HISTORY, PANTAGRAPH COLLECTION

DORIS DAY
YOUNG AT HEART
THE OUTCAST
NO PARKING
BUS ZONE
VELVET
FREEZE

ABOVE: Looking west on the 300 block of West Washington Street in 1962.
COURTESY OF THE MCLEAN COUNTY MUSEUM OF HISTORY, PANTAGRAPH COLLECTION

LEFT: A crew working on the National Bank Building in Bloomington, 1961.
COURTESY OF THE MCLEAN COUNTY MUSEUM OF HISTORY, PANTAGRAPH COLLECTION

OPPOSITE: Downtown Normal outside of the theater in 1958. COURTESY ILLINOIS STATE UNIVERSITY

ABOVE: Traffic backed up on Empire Street and Colton Avenue as Towanda Avenue closed for reconstruction, Bloomington, 1965.
COURTESY OF THE MCLEAN COUNTY MUSEUM OF HISTORY, PANTAGRAPH COLLECTION

ABOVE RIGHT: The McLean County Courthouse decorated for the Christmas parade that came by later that night, 1969.
COURTESY OF THE MCLEAN COUNTY MUSEUM OF HISTORY, PANTAGRAPH COLLECTION

RIGHT: Looking east on the 200 block of West Washington Street, March 20, 1965.
COURTESY OF THE MCLEAN COUNTY MUSEUM OF HISTORY, PANTAGRAPH COLLECTION

ABOVE: The Hotel Tilden Hall in Bloomington having its sign put back on in 1962.

COURTESY OF THE MCLEAN COUNTY MUSEUM OF HISTORY, PANTAGRAPH COLLECTION

LEFT: An aerial view of East Washington Street, Bloomington, 1969.

COURTESY OF THE MCLEAN COUNTY MUSEUM OF HISTORY, PANTAGRAPH COLLECTION

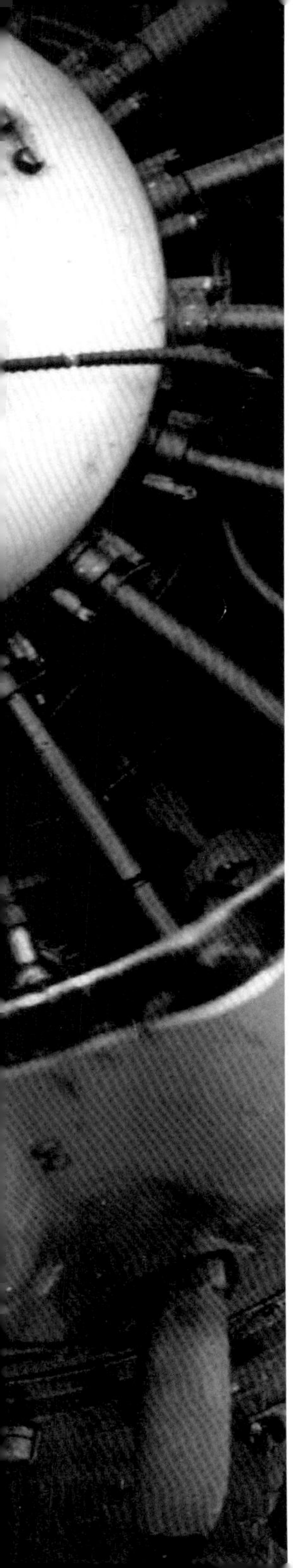

CHAPTER THREE

TRANSPORTATION

The Pantagraph's airplane, dubbed "Scoop," existed in several variations, and perhaps was the most visible example of how technology changed the Central Illinois landscape. The newspaper owned the airplane, which it sent up with a photographer to shoot landscape scenes and "big news," and to promote the company.

Houses were built to accommodate the must-have automobiles; car and truck dealerships (and the requisite filling stations and service garages) sat on many corners. Rail and air travel called for business dress; the family auto vacation was a mainstay, reflected in the nation's new interstate highway system and the millions of cars that traversed Route 66 from Chicago to California.

OPPOSITE: Art Carnahan, "Mr. Aviation," pictured with the Pantagraph's "Scoop IV," 1940. COURTESY DEB KING OCHS

ABOVE: SeaBees airplanes, which were able to land on a body of water as small as Lake Bloomington, circa 1944. COURTESY DEB KING OCHS

RIGHT: An Alton Railroad train, circa 1943.
COURTESY OF THE MCLEAN COUNTY MUSEUM OF HISTORY, PANTAGRAPH COLLECTION

OPPOSITE: Workmen reviving an Alton train so it could carry war supplies, 1943. To do this, they are taking out the flues, cleaning them, and fitting them back tightly.
COURTESY OF THE MCLEAN COUNTY MUSEUM OF HISTORY, PANTAGRAPH COLLECTION

RIGHT: A man trying to push a Chevrolet out of floodwaters, 1951. COURTESY OF THE MCLEAN COUNTY MUSEUM OF HISTORY, PANTAGRAPH COLLECTION

OPPOSITE TOP LEFT: William Oesch at Oesch transfer dock located on the corner of Oakland Avenue and East Street, 1942. COURTESY DON OESCH

OPPOSITE TOP RIGHT: An interurban bus that stopped at 1300 West Market Street on its way to Peoria, circa 1950. COURTESY BARBARA MCENTYRE

OPPOSITE BOTTOM LEFT: Hudson railroad depot located on Front Street, 1945. The station was constructed in 1854 and burned down in 1975. COURTESY HUDSON AREA PUBLIC LIBRARY

OPPOSITE BOTTOM RIGHT: A car trudging through 4.6 inches of floodwater on Lincoln Street, Bloomington, June of 1951. COURTESY OF THE MCLEAN COUNTY MUSEUM OF HISTORY, PANTAGRAPH COLLECTION

OESCH
OESCH
OESCH

278
COMPANY
278
TAXI
Peoples

HUDSON
GRAIN CO
HUDSON

ABOVE: A Brandt driver picking up a shipment of Beer Nuts at Shirk Products, 1963. COURTESY OF THE MCLEAN COUNTY MUSEUM OF HISTORY, PANTAGRAPH COLLECTION

ABOVE RIGHT: A man working on a bridge over U.S. 51, 1963. COURTESY OF THE MCLEAN COUNTY MUSEUM OF HISTORY, PANTAGRAPH COLLECTION

RIGHT: An Ozark DC-3 being inspected by curious citizens on Air Carrier Get Acquainted Day at Municipal Airport, 1951. It was a day where the plane was open to public viewing, and a few lucky citizens took a ride around Bloomington. COURTESY OF THE MCLEAN COUNTY MUSEUM OF HISTORY, PANTAGRAPH COLLECTION

OPPOSITE: Workers from the Eaton Asphalt Company putting blacktop on a Bloomington road in 1968. COURTESY OF THE MCLEAN COUNTY MUSEUM OF HISTORY, PANTAGRAPH COLLECTION

C
11

ABOVE: The Bloomington Airport terminal shop, circa 1964. COURTESY OF THE MCLEAN COUNTY MUSEUM OF HISTORY, PANTAGRAPH COLLECTION

ABOVE LEFT: An Illinois Central train wreck at Croxton Avenue in Bloominton, October 6, 1964. COURTESY BLOOMINGTON PUBLIC LIBRARY

LEFT: The Danvers Peoria and Eastern Railroad depot in 1965. COURTESY BLOOMINGTON PUBLIC LIBRARY

OPPOSITE: A Firestone worker inspecting the tread of a tire, 1968. COURTESY OF THE MCLEAN COUNTY MUSEUM OF HISTORY, PANTAGRAPH COLLECTION

CAPTAIN
ENGINE
3
1

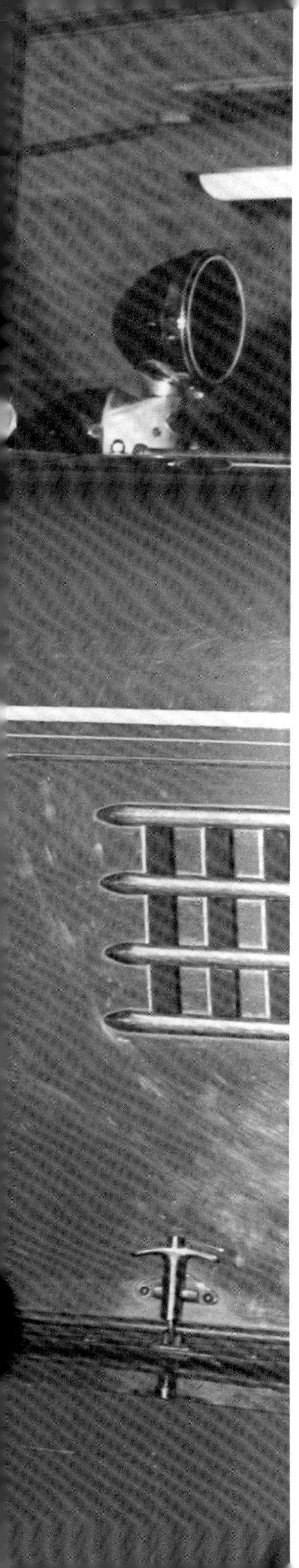

CHAPTER FOUR

PUBLIC SERVICE

Public service came into vogue in the 1940s after World War II. Fighting men returned home and communities proudly supported them as dedicated workers who kept the streets clean, sewers open, sidewalks swept, fires quelled, crime contained, trucks driven, railroads built and schools filled. Men and women had come to realize the importance of working for and helping others. Fire and police departments and other municipal services became more professionalized; they bought state-of-the-art equipment, trained in the newest techniques and proudly wore their uniforms. Hospitals and health care workers were everywhere, teaching the importance of vaccinations, cleanliness, personal hygiene and more, helping people who had grown up with outhouses, homemade soap and the notion that "doctoring" was saved for the most serious of injuries or illnesses.

OPPOSITE: Members of the Bloomington Fire Department in 1954. COURTESY OF THE MCLEAN COUNTY MUSEUM OF HISTORY, PANTAGRAPH COLLECTION

ABOVE: Clyde Kensinger inspecting the 250-watt transmitter ready for installation at the Bloomington Police Department, 1940.
COURTESY OF THE MCLEAN COUNTY MUSEUM OF HISTORY, PANTAGRAPH COLLECTION

ABOVE RIGHT: Riley Sizemore operating the switchboard at the generating plant in Bloomington, 1940. He was part of the water department. COURTESY OF THE MCLEAN COUNTY MUSEUM OF HISTORY, PANTAGRAPH COLLECTION

RIGHT: Sheriff Curtis Gilberts in the county jail's basement going through confiscated slot machines in 1947.
COURTESY OF THE MCLEAN COUNTY MUSEUM OF HISTORY, PANTAGRAPH COLLECTION

OPPOSITE: The Bloomington police force participating in training exercises, 1940.
COURTESY OF THE MCLEAN COUNTY MUSEUM OF HISTORY, PANTAGRAPH COLLECTION

ABOVE: The Bloomington Fire Department giving a demonstration of its new equipment in 1940.
COURTESY OF THE MCLEAN COUNTY MUSEUM OF HISTORY, PANTAGRAPH COLLECTION

LEFT: Firemen removing ice and snow from the S.S. Kresge Company building at 213 North Main Street, January 1, 1940. COURTESY OF THE MCLEAN COUNTY MUSEUM OF HISTORY, PANTAGRAPH COLLECTION

OPPOSITE: American Red Cross members of Bloomington, 1942.
COURTESY OF THE MCLEAN COUNTY MUSEUM OF HISTORY, PANTAGRAPH COLLECTION

ABOVE: A crowd listening to Dwight D. Eisenhower as he stops in Bloomington in 1952. COURTESY FUNK PRAIRIE HOME MUSEUM

RIGHT: Fred Winterroth running as a Republican candidate for the fourth ward, February 13, 1945. He was a politician in Bloomington until his retirement at age 77. COURTESY STAN WINTERROTH

FAR RIGHT: Herman Ochs, who served in the Pacific Theater as a cook, 1943. This photo was taken outside the Ko-Ko Shop, 114 North Street, Normal, which Louesa Ochs continued to run during Herman's service in New Caledonia. COURTESY DEB KING OCHS

ABOVE: A Bloomington City Council meeting in 1953.
COURTESY OF THE MCLEAN COUNTY MUSEUM OF HISTORY, PANTAGRAPH COLLECTION

LEFT: Governor Adlai Stevenson delivering an address at Bloomington's new armory on May 30, 1950. COURTESY OF THE MCLEAN COUNTY MUSEUM OF HISTORY, PANTAGRAPH COLLECTION

CITY HALL
WILLIAM H. DODSON
POST OFFICE
CAF

ABOVE: Captain Wendell Swearingen, left, helping Edwin Smiley with the pump, Bloomington Fire Department, 1957.
COURTESY OF THE MCLEAN COUNTY MUSEUM OF HISTORY, PANTAGRAPH COLLECTION

ABOVE LEFT: The Bloomington Fire Department in 1959. COURTESY OF THE MCLEAN COUNTY MUSEUM OF HISTORY, PANTAGRAPH COLLECTION

LEFT: American Red Cross members of Bloomington outside their chapter house at 709 East Douglas Street, 1957. COURTESY OF THE MCLEAN COUNTY MUSEUM OF HISTORY, PANTAGRAPH COLLECTION

OPPOSITE: Volunteers painting Bloomington's City Hall in 1956. COURTESY OF THE MCLEAN COUNTY MUSEUM OF HISTORY, PANTAGRAPH COLLECTION

ABOVE: Ronald Reagan speaking at the Bloomington Country Club on October 20, 1965. COURTESY OF THE MCLEAN COUNTY MUSEUM OF HISTORY, PANTAGRAPH COLLECTION

ABOVE RIGHT: Bloomington policemen standing next to their new squad car in 1961. James Alexander is on the left, and Douglas Bicknell is on the right. COURTESY OF THE MCLEAN COUNTY MUSEUM OF HISTORY, PANTAGRAPH COLLECTION

RIGHT: Bloomington postmen out delivering mail on January 18, 1962. COURTESY OF THE MCLEAN COUNTY MUSEUM OF HISTORY, PANTAGRAPH COLLECTION

OPPOSITE LEFT: Workers tearing up the streets for Bloomington's sewer project in 1962. The work started on Allin and Monroe Streets. COURTESY OF THE MCLEAN COUNTY MUSEUM OF HISTORY, PANTAGRAPH COLLECTION

OPPOSITE RIGHT: Frank Hartenstein breaking ground for the dedication of the new city hall building, 1961. COURTESY OF THE MCLEAN COUNTY MUSEUM OF HISTORY, PANTAGRAPH COLLECTION

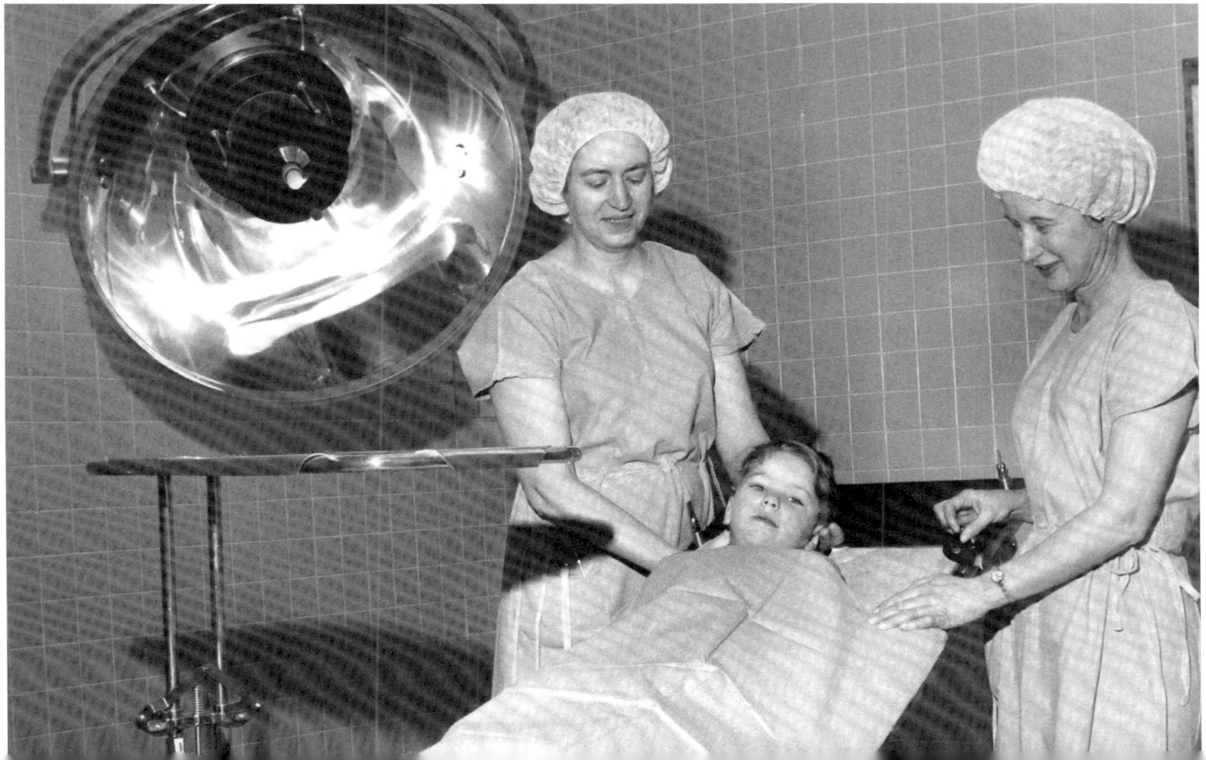

ABOVE: Firemen attempting to put out a blaze at the Terrace Restaurant on North Main Street, May 26, 1966.
COURTESY OF THE MCLEAN COUNTY MUSEUM OF HISTORY, PANTAGRAPH COLLECTION

ABOVE LEFT: Rufus Davis and his sons, Kim and Tracy, driving around Bloomington in their 1918 fire truck, circa 1965. Of course they had to make a stop at the fire department to show it off.
COURTESY OF THE MCLEAN COUNTY MUSEUM OF HISTORY, PANTAGRAPH COLLECTION

LEFT: The interior of St. Joseph's Hospital in 1968, where a little boy is waiting to have a procedure.
COURTESY OF THE MCLEAN COUNTY MUSEUM OF HISTORY, PANTAGRAPH COLLECTION

OPPOSITE: Bloomington firemen training, circa 1965.
COURTESY OF THE MCLEAN COUNTY MUSEUM OF HISTORY, PANTAGRAPH COLLECTION

RAPP'S
Welcomes
JACK DEM
Tide
KING SIZE
FREE INSIDE
4 juice cups
Scripto
BALL PEN

CHAPTER FIVE

COMMERCE

Business took off as salaries rose and the Great Depression faded into memory. Advances in technology and transportation brought more and cheaper goods from across the globe. In Central Illinois, agriculture and insurance led the way. Downtown business districts were common in every town, offering Saturday sales for families who "came to town" for a noon meal before a Sunday spent in church and with extended family. Dollar days, sidewalk sales and various promotions enticed shoppers with all manner of merchandise and gimmicks to get them inside. "Salesman" was a profession, not a slur.

Banks were key to it all, lending money to businesses to buy merchandise and to expand, lending money to families to buy houses or cars and offering ways to save, such as Christmas club accounts. Well-heeled businessmen aspired to join, or be asked to join, the local Chambers of Commerce.

OPPOSITE: Sharon Rapp Blunk and world heavyweight champion Jack Dempsey standing in front of Rapp's Market located on Empire and Madison streets, 1955. COURTESY DAVE BLUNK

ABOVE: Louesa and Herman Ochs, owners of The Ko-Ko Shop on 114 North Street, Normal, circa 1942. COURTESY DEB KING OCHS

ABOVE RIGHT: Workers and patrons at Miller Music, 419 North Main Street, 1946. From left: Ethell Phillips, Marguerite Burwitz, June Koerner, Lorene Miller and Mary Metzner. COURTESY FRANK R. MILLER

RIGHT: Johnson and Meihsner Gas Station, located at Locust and East streets, 1945. COURTESY MARTHA MEIHSNER GEISON

OPPOSITE: An interior view of Morrell's Cleaners and Furriers on Main and Empire streets, January 31, 1941. John Morrell was the owner. COURTESY OF THE MCLEAN COUNTY MUSEUM OF HISTORY, PANTAGRAPH COLLECTION

MORRELL'S
CLEANERS
FURRIERS

Kellogg's
RICE
KRISPIES
Kellogg's
RICE
KRISPIES
MODEL
SMOKING TOBACCO
7up
it likes you!
DAD'S
Dr.Pepp

ABOVE: Shoppers outside of Stamm's Good Clothes on Dollar Day, August 3, 1961.
COURTESY OF THE MCLEAN COUNTY MUSEUM OF HISTORY, PANTAGRAPH COLLECTION

ABOVE LEFT: Barber Clyde D. Hunter with his customer Irma Shepherd, November 26, 1958. COURTESY OF THE MCLEAN COUNTY MUSEUM OF HISTORY, PANTAGRAPH COLLECTION

LEFT: A Bloomington Association of Commerce event in 1952.
COURTESY OF THE MCLEAN COUNTY MUSEUM OF HISTORY, PANTAGRAPH COLLECTION

OPPOSITE: Youngsters outside of O'Neil Grocery on 1102 West Chestnut Street, September 12, 1948. At this point, the store had been housed in the same building for 79 years. COURTESY OF THE MCLEAN COUNTY MUSEUM OF HISTORY, PANTAGRAPH COLLECTION

ABOVE: A Bloomington store nearing capacity on Dollar Day, February 9, 1961. It was a day where stores downtown put on sales to bring in massive crowds. COURTESY OF THE MCLEAN COUNTY MUSEUM OF HISTORY, PANTAGRAPH COLLECTION

RIGHT: Remodeling underway at the Corn Belt Bank in Bloomington, September 14, 1961.
COURTESY OF THE MCLEAN COUNTY MUSEUM OF HISTORY, PANTAGRAPH COLLECTION

OPPOSITE: A crowd forming at Tilden Hall Hotel as H.S. Beeney auctions off bedding and fans, January 9, 1962. At this same auction, a baby grand piano sold for $300. COURTESY OF THE MCLEAN COUNTY MUSEUM OF HISTORY, PANTAGRAPH COLLECTION

THIS GOODYEAR
SURE-GRIP
WILL OUTPULL
CLAY DOOLEY
BLOOMINGTON

ABOVE: Switchboard operators for State Farm in 1963. They were in charge of getting calls to over 700 phones in two offices. COURTESY OF THE MCLEAN COUNTY MUSEUM OF HISTORY, PANTAGRAPH COLLECTION

OPPOSITE: Clay Dooley showing off a tire at his repair shop, February 12, 1965. COURTESY OF THE MCLEAN COUNTY MUSEUM OF HISTORY, PANTAGRAPH COLLECTION

RIGHT: Looking west on Washington Street where Paradise Cleaners is advertising its service for 88 cents, 1961.
COURTESY OF THE MCLEAN COUNTY MUSEUM OF HISTORY, PANTAGRAPH COLLECTION

OPPOSITE: State Farm employees hard at work at the East Oakland Avenue office, 1963.
COURTESY OF THE MCLEAN COUNTY MUSEUM OF HISTORY, PANTAGRAPH COLLECTION

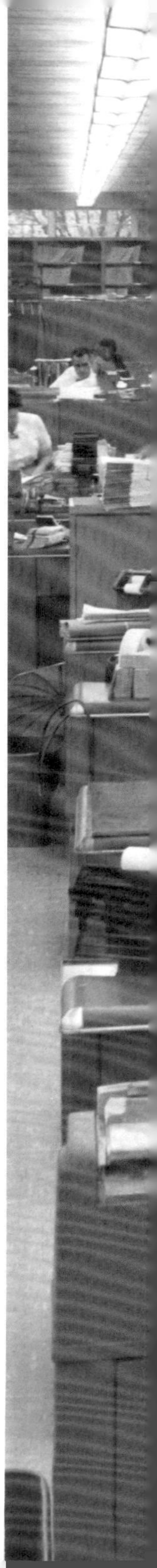

ABOVE: A man outside of Burton Baity Hardware in El Paso, 1969. COURTESY OF THE MCLEAN COUNTY MUSEUM OF HISTORY, PANTAGRAPH COLLECTION

ABOVE LEFT: A couple of cars parked in front of the State Bank of Gridley, circa 1968. COURTESY OF THE MCLEAN COUNTY MUSEUM OF HISTORY, PANTAGRAPH COLLECTION

LEFT: The grand opening of Beemer's Grocery Store, located on West Street in Hudson, 1966. COURTESY HUDSON AREA PUBLIC LIBRARY

BANNER BREAD
Oven Fresh
IGR
SAVE!
2-39

CHAPTER SIX

INDUSTRY AND AGRICULTURE

Corn, insurance and factories were the legs, (along with education, but more on that later), that held up McLean County for most of the 20th century. The flat land and black soil of Central Illinois proved one of the best places on earth to raise corn and soybeans, and a tremendous amount of research went into making hybrid seeds that would withstand the test of time.

State Farm, Country Companies (Illinois Farm Bureau companies), rail yards, coal companies and a vast number of production facilities made their homes in McLean County. Among other items, their workers made construction equipment, refrigerators, hair dryers, candy, electricity, vacuum cleaners, furnaces, baked goods, dairy goods, ice, coal, blankets, electrical parts and more.

OPPOSITE: A worker handling bread at Banner Bakery Company on 135 East Beaufort Street in Normal, 1963. It was a family company started by C.L. Keith Sr. COURTESY OF THE MCLEAN COUNTY MUSEUM OF HISTORY, PANTAGRAPH COLLECTION

ABOVE: A large crowd gathering on Farm Day, circa 1940.
COURTESY OF THE MCLEAN COUNTY MUSEUM OF HISTORY, PANTAGRAPH COLLECTION

RIGHT: Company K, Illinois Reserve Militia, assigned to Funk Brothers Seed Company, 1944. Included is Robert "Bob" Elkenberry. COURTESY JIM AND CONNIE TAYLOR

OPPOSITE: Funk Sr. and sons at Funk Farms in 1943. From left: LaFayette Funk, Gene Funk Jr., Paul Funk, Ted Funk, E.D. Funk Sr. COURTESY FUNK PRAIRIE HOME MUSEUM

FUNK FARMS
PROCESSING PLANT
FUNK'S HYBRID
SEED CORN

BLOOMINGTON
WE LIKE
IKE
IKE

ABOVE: Tracks and Ainsworth Ice Company building, located at 505 South McClun Street, circa 1944. It was operated by Hendra Lawrence Brown.
COURTESY DAVID L. BROWN

OPPOSITE: Gene Funk Jr., on the right, holding his family's hybrid corn with Les Arends while showing their support for Dwight D. Eisenhower in 1952.
COURTESY FUNK PRAIRIE HOME MUSEUM

ABOVE: Dr. J.R. Holbert, longtime research director and world-renowned corn breeder, at the Fall Research Harvest at Funk Seeds, 1947. COURTESY DENNY STEELE

RIGHT: Workers erecting the tower for WJBC in 1949.
COURTESY OF THE MCLEAN COUNTY MUSEUM OF HISTORY, PANTAGRAPH COLLECTION

OPPOSITE: People riding a corn detasseling machine, circa 1949.
COURTESY OF THE MCLEAN COUNTY MUSEUM OF HISTORY, PANTAGRAPH COLLECTION

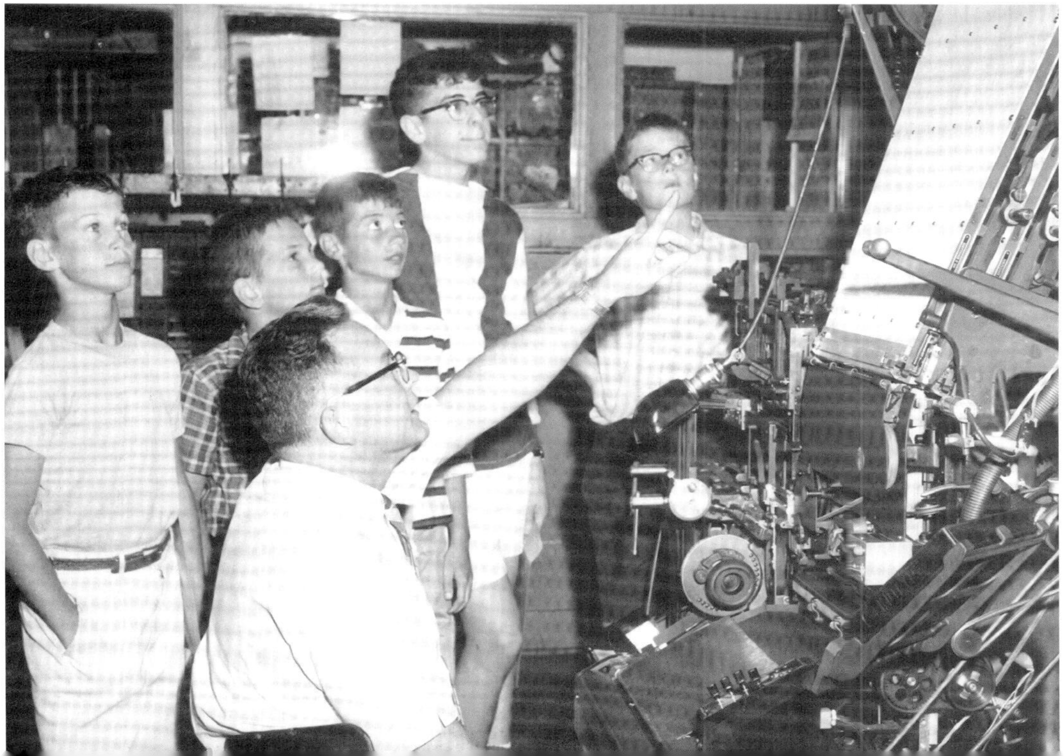

ABOVE: Lolita Driver, editor of Pantagraph's women's pages, circa 1958.
COURTESY OF THE MCLEAN COUNTY MUSEUM OF HISTORY, PANTAGRAPH COLLECTION

ABOVE LEFT: Rowe Construction employees working on a bulldozer at the Cottage Avenue garage in 1963.
COURTESY OF THE MCLEAN COUNTY MUSEUM OF HISTORY, PANTAGRAPH COLLECTION

LEFT: A linotype operator showing off the new equipment in the Pantagraph composing room, 1962.
COURTESY OF THE MCLEAN COUNTY MUSEUM OF HISTORY, PANTAGRAPH COLLECTION

OPPOSITE: Onlookers inspecting weed specimens on Farm Day in 1950. An estimated 7,000 attended. On the left is J.T. Rasmussen. Also included in the photograph are J.E. Barnes and Robert A. Evers.
COURTESY OF THE MCLEAN COUNTY MUSEUM OF HISTORY, PANTAGRAPH COLLECTION

ABOVE: Employees of Meadows Manufacturing Company, 1954.
COURTESY OF THE MCLEAN COUNTY MUSEUM OF HISTORY, PANTAGRAPH COLLECTION

ABOVE RIGHT: An employee of Watlington Manufacturing drilling holes into the dome of a hair dryer, 1963. They were located at 1204 North Linden Street.
COURTESY OF THE MCLEAN COUNTY MUSEUM OF HISTORY, PANTAGRAPH COLLECTION

RIGHT: Employees of Ma Girl Supply Company, circa 1963.
COURTESY OF THE MCLEAN COUNTY MUSEUM OF HISTORY, PANTAGRAPH COLLECTION

OPPOSITE: Workers at General Electric in 1954.
COURTESY OF THE MCLEAN COUNTY MUSEUM OF HISTORY, PANTAGRAPH COLLECTION

ARO
BALANCER
ARO
BALANCER

ABOVE: Bill Snyder showing off General Box Company's packages in 1963.
COURTESY OF THE MCLEAN COUNTY MUSEUM OF HISTORY, PANTAGRAPH COLLECTION

ABOVE LEFT: The Ralston Purina plant on Olive and Euclid streets, 1963.
COURTESY OF THE MCLEAN COUNTY MUSEUM OF HISTORY, PANTAGRAPH COLLECTION

LEFT: Workers at the packaging machine at Purity Baking Company, West Olive Street, 1963.
COURTESY OF THE MCLEAN COUNTY MUSEUM OF HISTORY, PANTAGRAPH COLLECTION

OPPOSITE: Workers outside of Illinois Power Company, which had over 130 employees in the Bloomington area alone, 1963. COURTESY OF THE MCLEAN COUNTY MUSEUM OF HISTORY, PANTAGRAPH COLLECTION

ABOVE LEFT: James Kiley working at Laesch Dairy on Morris Avenue, 1968. COURTESY OF THE MCLEAN COUNTY MUSEUM OF HISTORY, PANTAGRAPH COLLECTION

ABOVE MIDDLE: Workers at Automatic Tape Control after they merged with Gates Radio Company in 1966. COURTESY OF THE MCLEAN COUNTY MUSEUM OF HISTORY, PANTAGRAPH COLLECTION

ABOVE RIGHT: Tony Lammers checking vats at Unarco, 1111 West Perry Street, 1968. COURTESY OF THE MCLEAN COUNTY MUSEUM OF HISTORY, PANTAGRAPH COLLECTION

RIGHT: A crew of McLean County kids detasseling corn for Funk Seeds as a summer job, 1968. COURTESY DENNY STEELE

OPPOSITE: An Admiral Corporation employee sorting through their products, Morrissey Drive, 1963. COURTESY OF THE MCLEAN COUNTY MUSEUM OF HISTORY, PANTAGRAPH COLLECTION

Admiral

LEFT: An Alpha Cellulose Corporation employee moving a massive amount of product in 1963.

COURTESY OF THE MCLEAN COUNTY MUSEUM OF HISTORY, PANTAGRAPH COLLECTION

OPPOSITE TOP LEFT: Transformers ready to go up at the Co-Op building for Corn Belt Electric at the southeast edge of Bloomington, 1963.

COURTESY OF THE MCLEAN COUNTY MUSEUM OF HISTORY, PANTAGRAPH COLLECTION

OPPOSITE BOTTOM LEFT: Russell Shook doing motor tests for Eureka Company, circa 1968.

COURTESY OF THE MCLEAN COUNTY MUSEUM OF HISTORY, PANTAGRAPH COLLECTION

OPPOSITE RIGHT: Workers at K and K Engineering on 1016 East Grove Street, 1968.

COURTESY OF THE MCLEAN COUNTY MUSEUM OF HISTORY, PANTAGRAPH COLLECTION

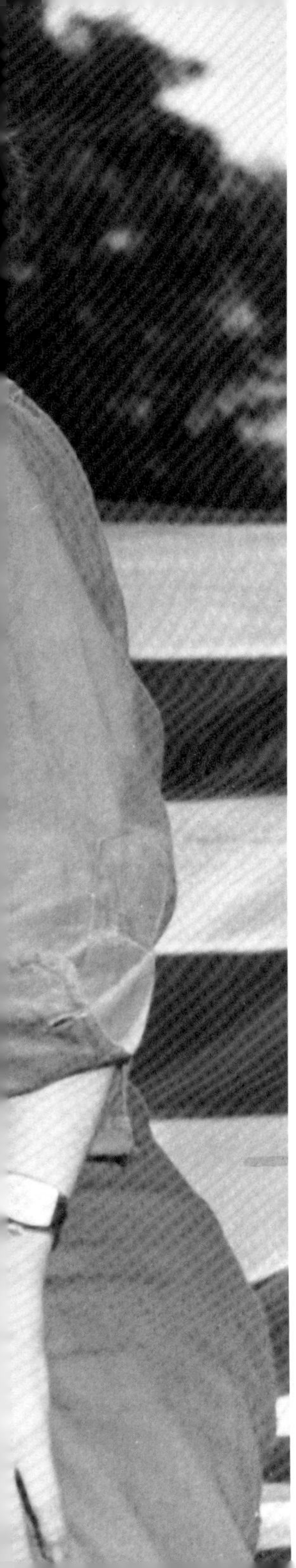

CHAPTER SEVEN

COMMUNITY

The people, of course, are what make a community into a welcoming home, and McLean County embodies this notion. With the common sense and caring that came naturally from the region's Midwestern character to the teachings carried out by hundreds of churches and religious bodies, McLean County residents helped each other and found joy through their work in a combination of service, faith-based and recreational groups, homeless shelters and organizations for abandoned or abused children.

In many respects, McLean County was like any other county in the country; in many other respects, it was not. Strong leadership from what became national businesses and nationally recognized schools, and from families whose members became national political leaders, helped keep eyes forward for many.

OPPOSITE: Two Bloomington Boy Scouts paying tribute to America in 1940. COURTESY OF THE MCLEAN COUNTY MUSEUM OF HISTORY, PANTAGRAPH COLLECTION

ABOVE: Boys exercising at the Bloomington YMCA, 1941.
COURTESY OF THE MCLEAN COUNTY MUSEUM OF HISTORY, PANTAGRAPH COLLECTION

RIGHT: A 1943 birthday party. First row from left: Don Powers, Carl Behr, Bob Mandler, Don Dexter, Tee Watson, Don Welsh, Denny Watson. Back row from left: Jack Rust, Don Cleary, Bill Costigon, Dewey, Welch, Hadley Sloan, Wendell Learned, Bill Brandt, Carter Wilson, Jim Ryan, Pete Elliott, Chalmers Elliott. COURTESY CARL BEHR

OPPOSITE: Modern dancers at the Bloomington YWCA, 1940. Selma Anderson is on the left, and LaVerne Young is on the right.
COURTESY OF THE MCLEAN COUNTY MUSEUM OF HISTORY, PANTAGRAPH COLLECTION

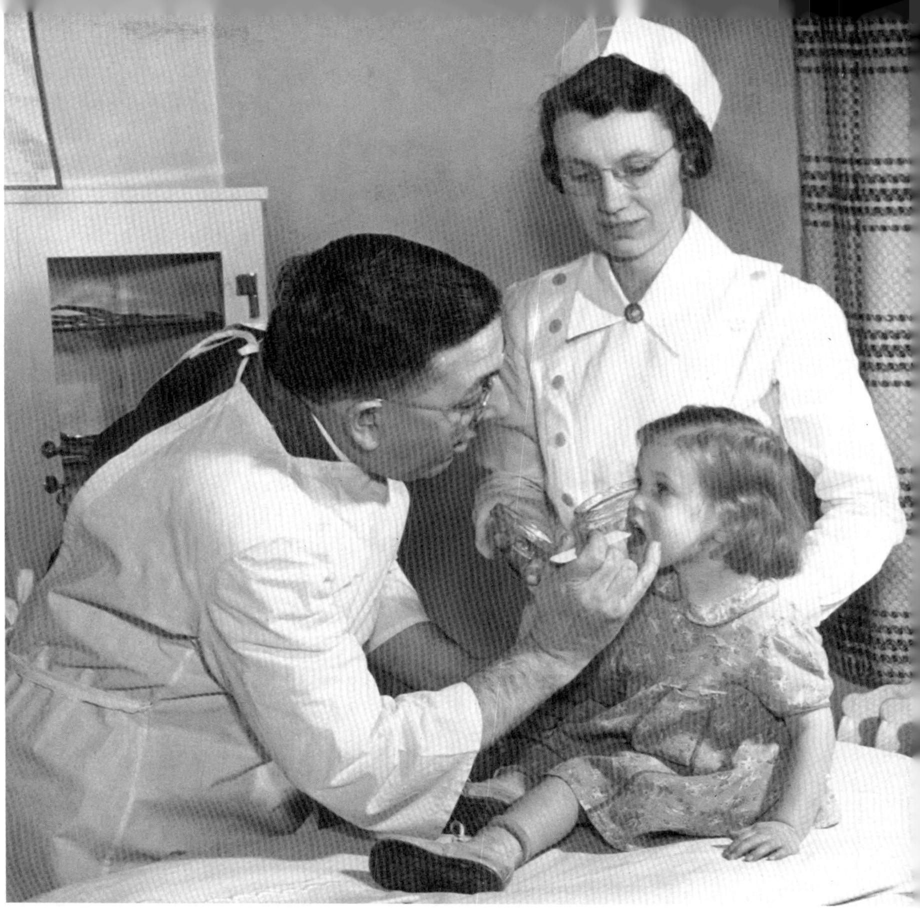

ABOVE: Dr. C. Carell Jones examining 2-year-old Lois Ann at the Normal Baby Fold after it was remodeled, 1940. COURTESY OF THE MCLEAN COUNTY MUSEUM OF HISTORY, PANTAGRAPH COLLECTION

ABOVE LEFT: Children of Hovey Avenue playing dress-up, circa 1945. Included in the photograph are Jann and Tommy Thompson, Lou and Paul Anderson Cook, and Davie and Stephen Denzer. COURTESY FRANK THOMPSON

LEFT: Dale Sutter, seated, and Daune Sutter, standing, display a miniature tractor made by their father, Merle Sutter, at a show of homemade farm labor-saving devices, 1947. COURTESY DALE M. SUTTER

OPPOSITE: First Communion at Saint Patrick's Rectory, circa 1947. Included in the photograph are Father Irish, Carol Smith Hoffman, John Deutch, Jim Ringle, Ronald Fogler, Marietta Shipley, Paul Bartosik, Carol Johnson and Fred Van Hook. COURTESY CAROL SMITH HOFFMAN

ABOVE: Reverend Doctor Harold Ray Martin giving a sermon at Second Presbyterian Church on East Street, circa 1955.
COURTESY HAROLD RAY BLEDSOE

ABOVE RIGHT: A Baby Fold cornerstone program event in 1950, which 750 people attended.
COURTESY OF THE MCLEAN COUNTY MUSEUM OF HISTORY, PANTAGRAPH COLLECTION

RIGHT: The ground-breaking ceremony at St. Matthew's Episcopal Church, August 1, 1954.
COURTESY OF THE MCLEAN COUNTY MUSEUM OF HISTORY, PANTAGRAPH COLLECTION

OPPOSITE: A full house listening to a sermon at Trinity Lutheran Church on South Madison Street, 1955.
COURTESY OF THE MCLEAN COUNTY MUSEUM OF HISTORY, PANTAGRAPH COLLECTION

SECOND PRESBYTERIAN
CHURCH
CHRISTIAN EDUCATION
BUILDING
1956

ABOVE: A view of the Chapel of the Templed Trees, about 300 feet into the woods near Funk Grove Church, 1956. Doctor Loyal M. Thompson can be seen in the walkway. COURTESY OF THE MCLEAN COUNTY MUSEUM OF HISTORY, PANTAGRAPH COLLECTION

ABOVE LEFT: Hudson Lion's Club Charter Night, 1964. COURTESY HUDSON AREA PUBLIC LIBRARY

LEFT: Boy Scouts campaigning for the vote in 1960.
COURTESY OF THE MCLEAN COUNTY MUSEUM OF HISTORY, PANTAGRAPH COLLECTION

OPPOSITE: People placing the cornerstone of Second Presbyterian Church's education building on 313 North East Street, 1956.
COURTESY OF THE MCLEAN COUNTY MUSEUM OF HISTORY, PANTAGRAPH COLLECTION

ABOVE LEFT: A cable toppling the tower of Trinity Lutheran on Madison and Olive Streets, 1962. The building had stood for seventy-eight years. COURTESY OF THE MCLEAN COUNTY MUSEUM OF HISTORY, PANTAGRAPH COLLECTION

ABOVE MIDDLE: Martin Wyckoff proudly displaying his Davey Crockett coonskin cap, circa 1956. The cap was donated to the McLean County Historical Society after his death in 2010. COURTESY SHARON WOLFE

ABOVE RIGHT: Martin Wyckoff with Santa Claus, circa 1960. COURTESY SHARON WOLFE

RIGHT: John Staszecki, who emigrated from Poland, lived at 1326 West Mulberry Street and was a coal miner, railroad worker, and wood worker, 1967. Shown here are a few of his carvings. COURTESY JOHN STASZECK

OPPOSITE: The Illinois 4-H Delegation at the National Congress, 1950. COURTESY GORDON ROPP

ILLINOIS
DELEGATION
National
4-H CLUB CONGRESS
1950

CHAPTER EIGHT

EDUCATION

McLean County became home to the state's newest teacher training school — a "normal" school — and what became Illinois State Normal University spawned the name of the town founded by Jesse Fell, who in his free time also founded The Pantagraph and is credited with putting Abe Lincoln's name into nomination for the presidency.

Education had become a way of leveling the field between immigrants and those whose families had been in America for a long time. With the advent of ISNU, and Illinois Wesleyan University, the importance and availability of education at all levels was a central strength of McLean County. The identities of smaller towns often hinged on having a school, a post office and a bank; bragging rights among school sports teams brought community pride with every football, basketball or baseball tossed.

OPPOSITE: The Illinois State Normal University homecoming parade in 1957. COURTESY ILLINOIS STATE UNIVERSITY

ABOVE: Trinity Lutheran School students in 1945.
COURTESY OF THE MCLEAN COUNTY MUSEUM OF HISTORY, PANTAGRAPH COLLECTION

ABOVE RIGHT: Students of Ben Funk School, 1940.
COURTESY FUNK PRAIRIE HOME MUSEUM

RIGHT: Students at Sheridan School dedicating their new flagpole on April 15, 1941.
COURTESY OF THE MCLEAN COUNTY MUSEUM OF HISTORY, PANTAGRAPH COLLECTION

OPPOSITE: Illinois Wesleyan students on their homecoming float, 1940. COURTESY TATE ARCHIVES & SPECIAL COLLECTIONS, THE AMES LIBRARY, ILLINOIS WESLEYAN UNIVERSITY, BLOOMINGTON, ILLINOIS

I.W.U.
90TH
ANNIV.
AMERICA LIBERTY
WESLEYAN VICTORY
DELTA
OMICRON

ABOVE: Donna West Mildner, center, and two other Lexington High School cheerleaders, circa 1945. COURTESY RICK GOODE

LEFT: Fourth-grade students of Thomas Metcalf Elementary School selling lemonade as a business exercise, 1949. Included in the photograph are Fage Mansfield, Deddie Hill, Carol Gimstead, Chip McKnight, Tommy Thompson, Alec Wode and Gordon Groves. COURTESY FRANK THOMPSON

OPPOSITE: Eighth-grade class of Bent School, located on West Walnut Street, 1942. COURTESY DAVE MURRAY

ABOVE: Illinois Wesleyan University students competing in a rope-pulling competition on homecoming, 1955.
COURTESY TATE ARCHIVES & SPECIAL COLLECTIONS, THE AMES LIBRARY, ILLINOIS WESLEYAN UNIVERSITY, BLOOMINGTON, ILLINOIS

RIGHT: Illinois Wesleyan University's Independent Women Club, 1950.
COURTESY TATE ARCHIVES & SPECIAL COLLECTIONS, THE AMES LIBRARY, ILLINOIS WESLEYAN UNIVERSITY, BLOOMINGTON, ILLINOIS

OPPOSITE: The Illinois Wesleyan University centennial celebration in 1950. COURTESY TATE ARCHIVES & SPECIAL COLLECTIONS, THE AMES LIBRARY, ILLINOIS WESLEYAN UNIVERSITY, BLOOMINGTON, ILLINOIS

1850
WESLEYAN
SCIENTIA
ET
1950

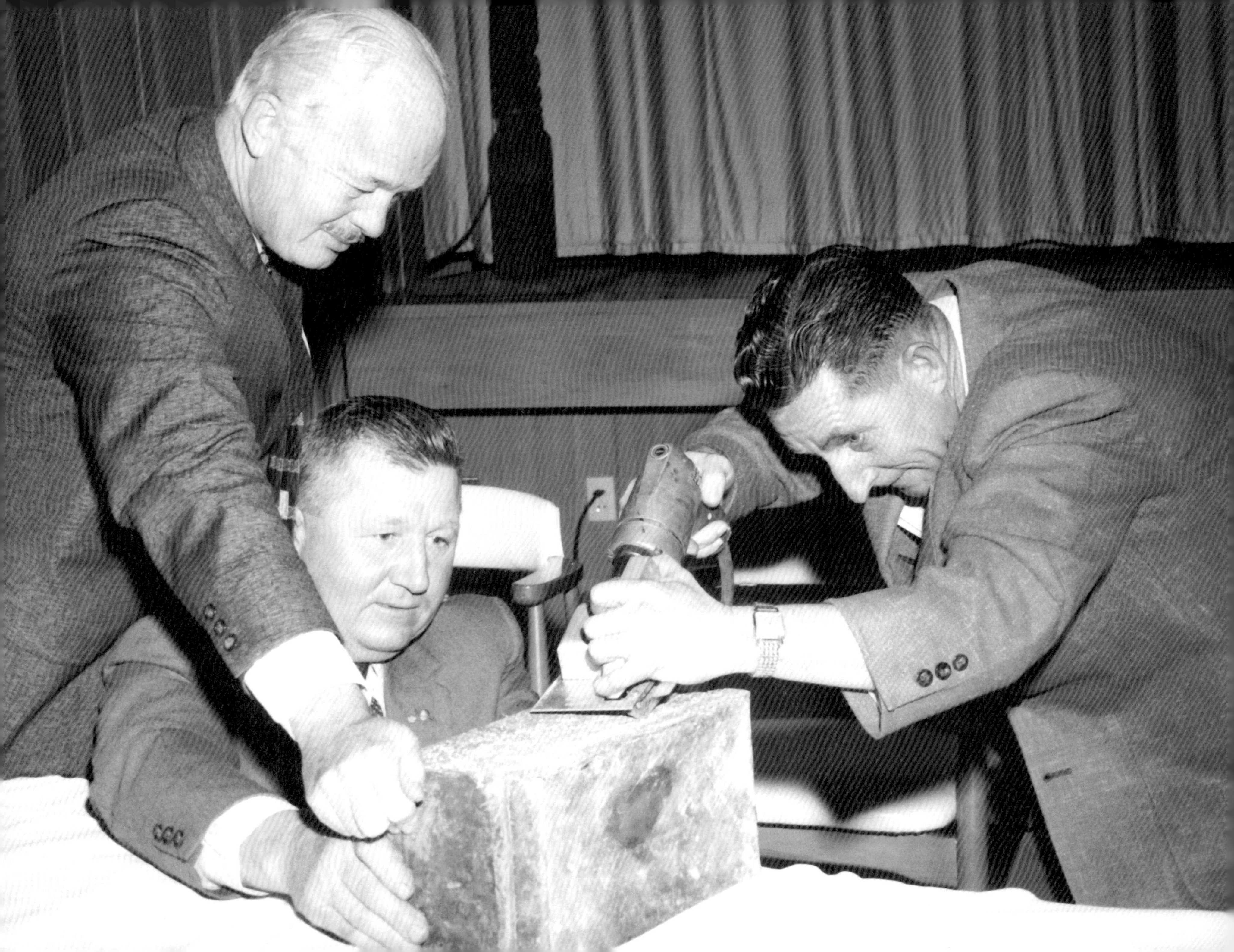

ABOVE: Eighth-grade graduation at Saint Patrick's Grade School, 1955. Front row, from left: Lucy Einhorn, Marietta Shipley, Carol Smith Hoffman. Middle row, from left: Roberta Gustavson, Carol Johnson, Mollie Frisch, Phyllis Foreman. Back row: Regins Berberet, Paul Bartosik, Elmo Kistner, James Ringel, Father John Ring. COURTESY CAROL SMITH HOFFMAN

ABOVE LEFT: Illinois State Normal University cheerleaders in 1956. COURTESY ILLINOIS STATE UNIVERSITY

LEFT: Lexington's 1954 homecoming dance. COURTESY RICK GOODE

OPPOSITE: Illinois State Normal University President Robert G. Bone and Clarence Ropp watching as the cornerstone of Old Main was broken, 1957. COURTESY RAY ROPP

5:00 A.M.
SPEED LIMIT 20
Coachman
MOTEL-DINING
ILLINOIS STATE UNIVERSIT
HOTEL
WALDORF
SANDWICH BAR

42
12
24
20

79
57

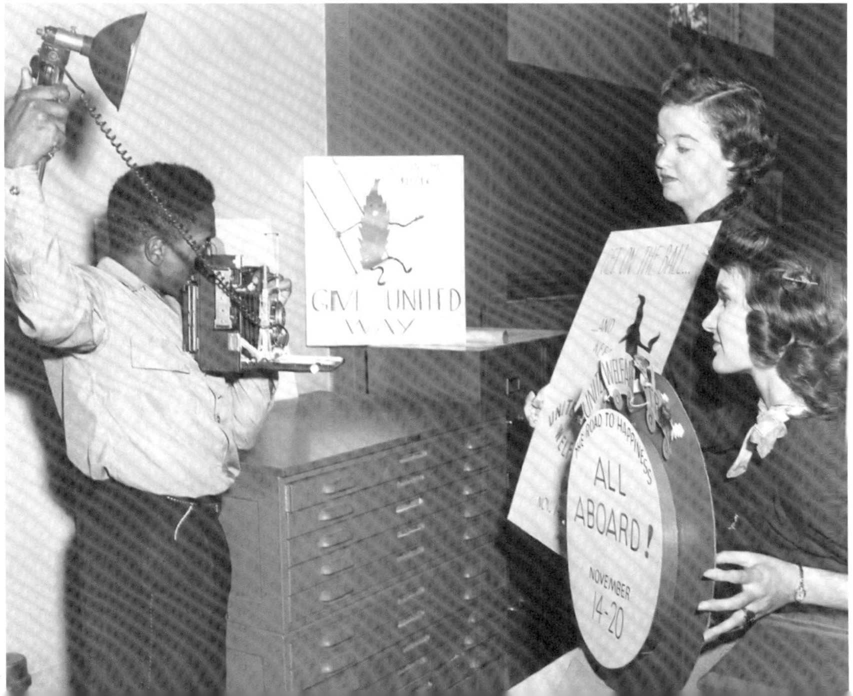

ABOVE: The fourth-, fifth-, and sixth-grade basketball team of Colfax Grade School, 1957. Included in the photograph are Jim Taylor and Coach Paul Henkel. COURTESY JIM AND CONNIE TAYLOR

LEFT: Students shooting advertisements for the Bloomington Junior High School paper, 1954. COURTESY OF THE MCLEAN COUNTY MUSEUM OF HISTORY, PANTAGRAPH COLLECTION

OPPOSITE TOP LEFT: Students setting up decorations for Illinois State University in 1965. COURTESY ILLINOIS STATE UNIVERSITY

OPPOSITE TOP RIGHT: A mid-air collision at an Illinois Wesleyan University basketball game, circa 1963. COURTESY TATE ARCHIVES & SPECIAL COLLECTIONS, THE AMES LIBRARY, ILLINOIS WESLEYAN UNIVERSITY, BLOOMINGTON, ILLINOIS

OPPOSITE BOTTOM LEFT: The 10-year reunion of Bloomington High School class of 1959, located on East Washington Street, 1969. COURTESY RUTH STEWART

OPPOSITE BOTTOM RIGHT: A muddy Illinois State Normal University football game in 1958. COURTESY ILLINOIS STATE UNIVERSITY

ABOVE LEFT: Former Illinois State Normal University President Dr. Robert G. Bone carrying books in 1961. He did this in preparation for a contest where the highest bidder would get to have Bone carry their books around campus. Included in the photograph are Linda Sweetin, Sammie Day and Pearl Henderson.
COURTESY OF THE MCLEAN COUNTY MUSEUM OF HISTORY, PANTAGRAPH COLLECTION

ABOVE RIGHT: Students getting off of the Bloomington High School bus in 1959.
COURTESY OF THE MCLEAN COUNTY MUSEUM OF HISTORY, PANTAGRAPH COLLECTION

RIGHT: Reverend Doctor Martin Luther King Jr. speaking on the Illinois Wesleyan University campus on February 2, 1966. Behind him are Coretta Scott King and Elizabeth Lindblom.
COURTESY TATE ARCHIVES & SPECIAL COLLECTIONS, THE AMES LIBRARY, ILLINOIS WESLEYAN UNIVERSITY, BLOOMINGTON, ILLINOIS

ABOVE: Lunch time at Bloomington High School in 1959. COURTESY OF THE MCLEAN COUNTY MUSEUM OF HISTORY, PANTAGRAPH COLLECTION

ABOVE LEFT: The Mennonite Hospital School of Nursing class of 1960. COURTESY DELORIS CARTER

LEFT: Seventh- and eighth-grade girls dressed in Dominican sister's habits at Saint Patrick's Grade School, 1957. COURTESY CAROL SMITH HOFFMAN

STATE FARM
DAY CAMP

CHAPTER NINE

RECREATION AND CELEBRATIONS

The 1940s, '50s and '60s remained mainly unchanged in Central Illinois, with little hint of the national uproar to come over the Vietnam War, the Equal Rights Amendment, Roe v. Wade, Watergate, Title IX and other social changes. Instead, in that middle part of the 20th century, McLean County kept a strong focus on "healthy" recreation (fishing, swimming, skating and school parties) and parades to mark the centennial anniversaries of our towns and schools. In times of national celebration (victory in war) and grief (the deaths of presidents), McLean County stood as one to mark the occasions.

OPPOSITE: A fishing competition at G.J. Mecherle Memorial Park, circa 1950. Included in the photograph are Carol Ann Smith Hoffman and John Smith.
COURTESY CAROL SMITH HOFFMAN

ABOVE: Boys playing with model airplanes near Bloomington, 1945. COURTESY OF THE MCLEAN COUNTY MUSEUM OF HISTORY, PANTAGRAPH COLLECTION

ABOVE RIGHT: The Rae Ann dance group of 1949. Included in the photograph are Carol Orrick, Nancy Menken, Helen Johnson, Janet Hayslip, Ruth Riedel, and Dorita Durbin. COURTESY RUTH STEWART

RIGHT: A band marching down South Main Street in Bloomington in a Memorial Day Parade, 1950. Included in the photograph are Mabel Hileman and Harold Hileman. COURTESY SUZANNE KAHL

OPPOSITE: The Chicago Stockyards visiting Bloomington for the Thanksgiving Corn Bowl game between Southern Illinois and North Central College, 1947. COURTESY OF THE MCLEAN COUNTY MUSEUM OF HISTORY, PANTAGRAPH COLLECTION

CHICAGO STOCKYARDS
POST
333
AMERICAN
U.S.
LEGION
DEPT OF ILLINOIS
AMERICAN LEGION

BLOOMING GROVE OR BUST

LEFT: Carl and Dorothy Durbin performing their circus routine in 1950.
COURTESY OF THE MCLEAN COUNTY MUSEUM OF HISTORY, PANTAGRAPH COLLECTION

OPPOSITE LEFT: The Frank Thompson family on one of their many camping trips, circa 1950. COURTESY FRANK THOMPSON

OPPOSITE TOP RIGHT: Groups of boys canoeing on Lake Bloomington, 1951.
COURTESY OF THE MCLEAN COUNTY MUSEUM OF HISTORY, PANTAGRAPH COLLECTION

OPPOSITE BOTTOM RIGHT: Oakland School's float for the Bloomington Centennial Parade, September 20, 1950.
COURTESY OF THE MCLEAN COUNTY MUSEUM OF HISTORY, PANTAGRAPH COLLECTION

ABOVE: The 1954 little league baseball team of Lexington. COURTESY RICK GOODE

OPPOSITE: The softball champions of Silver Leaf Let's Go Agriculture 4-H club, 1960. COURTESY RAY ROPP

AUTO-LITE
SERVICE

LEFT: The Bloomington Municipal Band playing at Miller Park in the summer of 1961. Chester C. Hamilton was the director.

COURTESY OF THE MCLEAN COUNTY MUSEUM OF HISTORY, PANTAGRAPH COLLECTION

BELOW LEFT: A band playing at Miller Park on June 20, 1958.

COURTESY OF THE MCLEAN COUNTY MUSEUM OF HISTORY, PANTAGRAPH COLLECTION

OPPOSITE: Mayor Robert McGraw giving a speech at the dedication of the new City Hall, November 11, 1961.

COURTESY OF THE MCLEAN COUNTY MUSEUM OF HISTORY, PANTAGRAPH COLLECTION

REFRESHMENTS

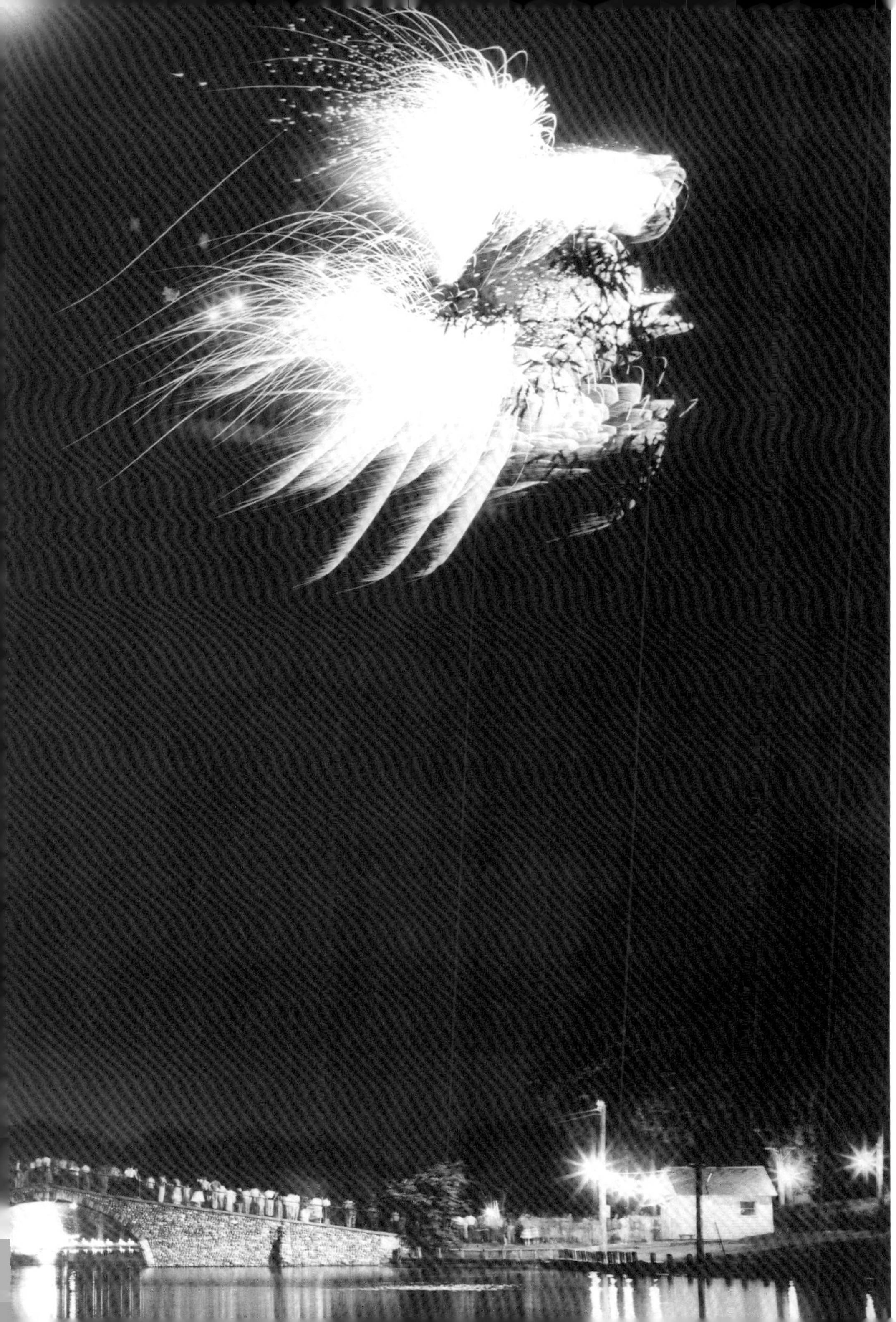

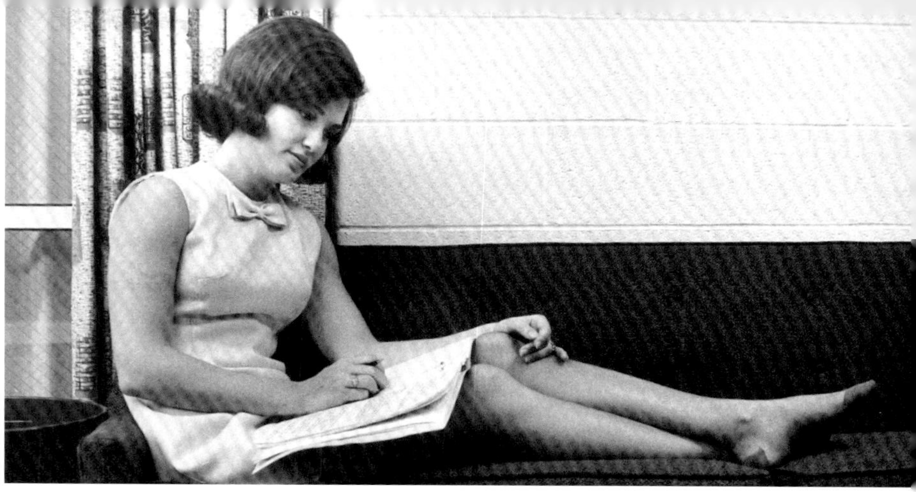

ABOVE: Lea Ann Miller, Cindy Miller, and Harold Miller Jr. in a miniature steam railroad caboose at Miller Park Zoo, July 1957. COURTESY AMY MILLER

TOP: Anita Gibb studying in 1968, the year she was crowned Miss McLean. COURTESY OF THE MCLEAN COUNTY MUSEUM OF HISTORY, PANTAGRAPH COLLECTION

LEFT: The fireworks display on July 4, 1957, at Miller Park. COURTESY OF THE MCLEAN COUNTY MUSEUM OF HISTORY, PANTAGRAPH COLLECTION

OPPOSITE: People enjoying Miller Park and the new ski slide, 1961. COURTESY OF THE MCLEAN COUNTY MUSEUM OF HISTORY, PANTAGRAPH COLLECTION

ABOVE: People enjoying the Four Seasons' new indoor skating rink, 1962. COURTESY OF THE MCLEAN COUNTY MUSEUM OF HISTORY, PANTAGRAPH COLLECTION

ABOVE RIGHT: The new gas pump on Lake Bloomington, 1964. It was put there because the city raised the limit on horsepower, which brought more people to the lake. COURTESY OF THE MCLEAN COUNTY MUSEUM OF HISTORY, PANTAGRAPH COLLECTION

RIGHT: People cooling off at the Miller Park swimming pool while the Soap Box Derby was underway nearby, 1965. COURTESY OF THE MCLEAN COUNTY MUSEUM OF HISTORY, PANTAGRAPH COLLECTION

OPPOSITE: After heavy rains pushed fish into the swimming area at Miller Park, these boys were catching them with their bare hands, 1964. From left: Stanley Griffin, Kenneth Sylvester, Michael Hickman, Roger Carey. COURTESY OF THE MCLEAN COUNTY MUSEUM OF HISTORY, PANTAGRAPH COLLECTION

INDEX

We're proud to call
McLean County home.
COUNTRY
FINANCIAL®
GROWMARK

Over

90 YEARS

1920 2016

of Community Banking

hbtbank.com | 888-897-2276

Heartland Bank and Trust Company

MEMBER FDIC

El Paso National Bank, purchased in 1964 by George Drake and other investors

The Heartland Bank Tradition

The strength of our bank lies in the relationships that give meaning to our work. At all times, we remain focused on what we do best: Operating as a dependable community bank and delivering on our personal service commitment.

This compassionate approach originated with M.B. Drake, who started the family banking tradition in 1920. M.B. was famous for reminding everyone, *"It's nice to be important, but it's more important to be nice."* Those words still ring true today.

Following military service in World War II and graduation from the University of Illinois, one of M.B.'s sons, George, began his banking career, one that lasted over 50 years! In 1964, he and other investors purchased a small bank in El Paso, Illinois – and so began what would eventually become Heartland Bank and Trust Company. George remains an active Heartland Bank board member.

Two of George's sons, also University of Illinois graduates, joined George in the family banking business. Allen, now retired, held several leadership positions at Heartland Bank and still serves on its board of directors. Fred began working part-time at the bank during high school. After obtaining his undergraduate degree in Finance and his MBA, Fred began his successful banking career in 1980.

It's nice to be important,
but it's more important to be nice.
- M.B. Drake

Since 1992, Fred has guided Heartland Bank through continuous years of strong earnings and market expansion. As Chairman and CEO of Heartland Bancorp, Inc., Fred continues to focus on leading the bank's overall strategy, seeking new opportunities, and ensuring the bank's continued success. Heartland Bank and Trust Company is an independently owned community bank with assets of $3 billion. Headquartered in Bloomington, IL, the bank has offices in communities throughout Illinois.

Explore 150 years of history as it originally appeared

Pages from our past

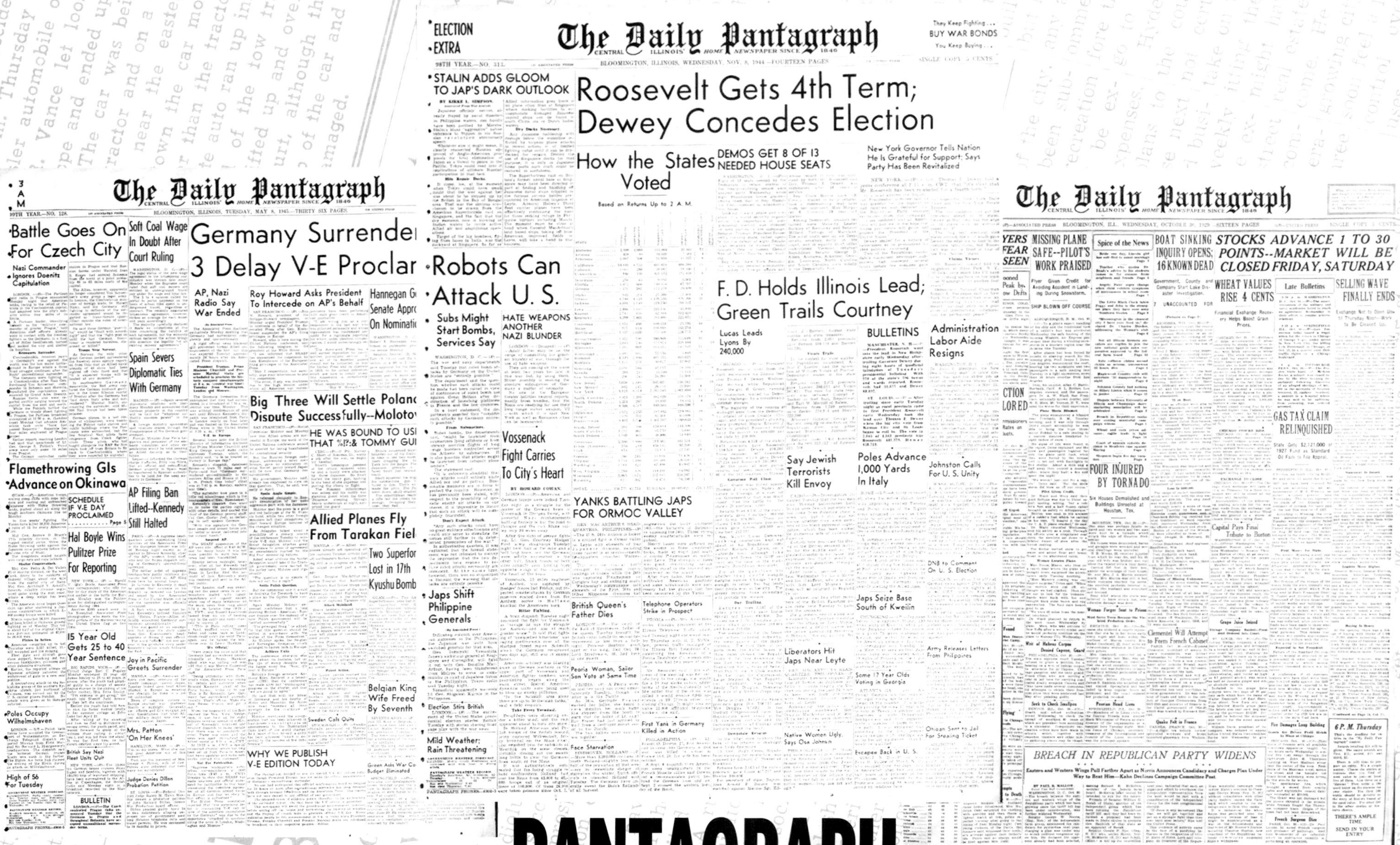

ELECTION EXTRA

The Daily Pantagraph — Central Illinois' Home Newspaper Since 1846

They Keep Fighting ... BUY WAR BONDS You Keep Buying ...

98TH YEAR—NO. 312. BLOOMINGTON, ILLINOIS, WEDNESDAY, NOV. 8, 1944—FOURTEEN PAGES

Roosevelt Gets 4th Term; Dewey Concedes Election

STALIN ADDS GLOOM TO JAP'S DARK OUTLOOK

How the States Voted

Based on Returns Up to 2 A.M.

DEMOS GET 8 OF 13 NEEDED HOUSE SEATS

New York Governor Tells Nation He Is Grateful for Support; Says Party Has Been Revitalized

Robots Can Attack U. S.

Subs Might Start Bombs, Services Say

HATE WEAPONS ANOTHER NAZI BLUNDER

F. D. Holds Illinois Lead; Green Trails Courtney

Lucas Leads Lyons By 240,000

BULLETINS

Administration Labor Aide Resigns

Vossenack Fight Carries To City's Heart

YANKS BATTLING JAPS FOR ORMOC VALLEY

Say Jewish Terrorists Kill Envoy

Poles Advance 1,000 Yards In Italy

Johnston Calls For U. S. Unity

DNB to Comment On U. S. Election

Japs Shift Philippine Generals

British Queen's Father Dies

Telephone Operators Strike in Prospect

Liberators Hit Japs Near Leyte

Japs Seize Base South of Kweilin

Army Releases Letters From Philippines

Election Stirs British

Peoria Woman, Sailor Son Vote at Same Time

Some 17 Year Olds Voting in Georgia

Mild Weather; Rain Threatening

Face Starvation

First Yanks in Germany Killed in Action

Native Women Ugly, Says Osa Johnson

Onoan Sent to Jail For Stealing Ticket

Escapee Back in U. S.

The Daily Pantagraph — Central Illinois' Home Newspaper Since 1846

3 A.M.

99TH YEAR—NO. 128. BLOOMINGTON, ILLINOIS, TUESDAY, MAY 8, 1945.—THIRTY SIX PAGES.

Battle Goes On For Czech City

Nazi Commander Ignores Doenitz Capitulation

Soft Coal Wage In Doubt After Court Ruling

Germany Surrenders; 3 Delay V-E Proclamation

AP, Nazi Radio Say War Ended

Roy Howard Asks President To Intercede on AP's Behalf

Hannegan Gets Senate Approval On Nomination

Spain Severs Diplomatic Ties With Germany

Big Three Will Settle Poland Dispute Successfully—Molotov

HE WAS BOUND TO USE THAT %!?:& TOMMY GUN

Flamethrowing GIs Advance on Okinawa

SCHEDULE IF V-E DAY PROCLAIMED

AP Filing Ban Lifted—Kennedy Still Halted

Allied Planes Fly From Tarakan Field

Hal Boyle Wins Pulitzer Prize For Reporting

Two Superfortresses Lost in 17th Kyushu Bombing

15 Year Old Gets 25 to 40 Year Sentence

Joy in Pacific Greets Surrender

Belgian King's Wife Freed By Seventh

Poles Occupy Wilhelmshaven

Mrs. Patton 'On Her Knees'

Sweden Calls Quits

British Say Nazi Fleet Units Quit

High of 56 For Tuesday

Judge Denies Dillon Probation Petition

BULLETIN

WHY WE PUBLISH V-E EDITION TODAY

The Daily Pantagraph — Central Illinois' Home Newspaper Since 1846

BLOOMINGTON, ILL., WEDNESDAY, OCTOBER 30, 1929—SIXTEEN PAGES

MISSING PLANE SAFE—PILOT'S WORK PRAISED

Spice of the News

BOAT SINKING INQUIRY OPENS; 16 KNOWN DEAD

STOCKS ADVANCE 1 TO 30 POINTS—MARKET WILL BE CLOSED FRIDAY, SATURDAY

WHEAT VALUES RISE 4 CENTS

Late Bulletins

SELLING WAVE FINALLY ENDS

GAS TAX CLAIM RELINQUISHED

FOUR INJURED BY TORNADO

Capital Pays Final Tribute to Burton

Clemenceau Will Attempt to Form French Cabinet

BREACH IN REPUBLICAN PARTY WIDENS

6 P. M. Thursday

THE PANTAGRAPH

pantagraph.com

Pages from our past

The Daily Pantagraph.

BLOOMINGTON, ILL. MONDAY MORNING, FEBRUARY 14, 1910.—TWELVE PAGES.

SELL YOUR STOCK — 15 Words 3 Times 30 Cents

SECOND-HAND MACHINERY — 15 Words 3 Times 30 Cents

RIOTS IN GERMANY

Socialists Clash With Police in Many Cities Thruout the Kingdom.

STATE BOARD WILL ACT

POSED FOR A SKETCH

This, With Reception of Two Callers, Occupied President Sunday.

GIRL IS CUT TO PIECES.

DISCOVER NEW LAND.

MADRID IS RETICENT.

MAY DROP SUBSIDY

President is Not Expected to Bring Pressure to Bear on Measure.

BRITAIN HAS AIRSHIP.

DEATH SENTENCE CHEERED

DEFEAT FOR ROOT PLAN

IS RAISULI DEAD?

FAIRBANKS IS NOT BLAMED

BANDIT JOINS POSSE.

FACE HERESY CHARGES.

DIFFER AS TO THE TARIFF

HOLDS CONTRACT ILLEGAL

RECEIVER FOR A FOUNDRY

CRUISER TO THE RESCUE

GAS FIX URES LEAKED.

NEW PARTY IS URGED.

SELLS STAMPS FACE DOWN

RESUME MEAT PROBE TODAY

WILL "REMEMBER THE MAINE"

DR. COOK IS LOCATED.

TEETHING CAUSES DEATH

PULLMAN INTO THE RIVER

CONVICT IS HEIR TO $80,000

COLD WAVE IS PREDICTED

OFFICER SHOT DEAD.

FORGES FOR HIS ROBES

LATONIA TRACK SOLD.

JURORS CANNOT AGREE

MUCH FRUIT BURNED

TELEGRAPHIC FLASHES.

The Daily Pantagraph.

Germans Will Soon Meet the ...

GERMAN FORCE IS PUSHING FORWARD

BELGIANS STILL HOLD LIEGE FORTS

GERMANS LEFT PILES OF DEAD

JAPAN TO FIGHT

WILL SEND HOSPITAL SHIP

JOINS FRENCH REGIMENT

CAPTURED 700 UHLANS

OFFICERS ARE EXCHANGED

STILL IN DARDANELLES

TURKEY REMAINS NEUTRAL

GERMAN OFFICERS REMAIN

The Daily Pantagraph — Central Illinois' Home Newspaper Since 1846

BLOOMINGTON, ILL., THURSDAY, AUG. 16, 1945.—FOURTEEN PAGES.

They Won the Battles ... WIN THE PEACE You Do Your Share Now

Gaining Prosperous Peace Now Job Facing Nation

230 Unexploded Jap Bombs Lying In Western U. S.

Found Innocent Of Crime After Serving Term

Here's Complete Picture Of Nation as It Faces Work of Reconversion

Omit Steak on Menus Yet; Shortages Still With Us

All Services To Free Vets In a Hurry

5 More Divisions Coming Home!

No Word From Japs On Surrender Plan

MacArthur Reports 'No Reply' Yet

CLOSED STORES ADVISED TO OPEN UP

Illinois Central Sets Strike Date For 1,800

Atom Bomb Production Still Going

Boys Confess Hanging 7 Year Old

Communists Turn Down Chiang's Rule

Youths Drown While Wading To Shore

Doubts If DDT Will Halt Polio

Imprisonment Almost Sure For Petain

Adopted Children Fight Will

4 Hurt in VJ Celebration

Horse's Kick Kills Farmer

Arnold Lauds All in Air Force

Fisherman Drowns in River

Day of Ample Clothing Still 4 to 6 Months Away

THE PANTAGRAPH

pantagraph.com